ROYAL COUR

CW00548266

The Royal Court Theatre presents

GOODBYE TO ALL THAT

by **Luke Norris**

GOODBYE TO ALL THAT was first performed at The Royal Court Jerwood Theatre Upstairs, Sloane Square, on Thursday 23rd February 2012.

Principal Sponsor

GOODBYE TO ALL THAT

by Luke Norris

David **Alexander Cobb**
Frank **Roger Sloman**
Rita **Linda Marlowe**
Iris **Susan Brown**

Director **Simon Godwin**
Designer **Tom Piper**
Lighting Designer **Matt Drury**
Sound Designer **Alexander Caplen**
Casting Director **Amy Ball**
Assistant Director **Alice Lacey**
Production Manager **Tariq Rifaat**
Stage Managers **Sarah Hellicar, Alison Rich**
Stage Management Work Placement **Claire Bradley**
Costume Supervisor **Iona Kenrick**
Choreography **Lootie Johansen-Bibby**
Set Builders **Object Construction**
Scenic Painter **Jodie Pritchard**
Assistant Scenic Painter **Hannah Baker**

The Royal Court and Stage Management wish to thank the following for their help with this
production: Tricycle Theatre, Donmar Warehouse, Almeida Theatre, Guildford School of
Acting, Yvonne Arnaud Theatre, Royal Marsden Hospital, Milton Keynes General Hospital,
Romford Golf Club, Hampstead Theatre, Southwood Golf Club, Marie Askin, University of
Leicester, Curtain Craft Ltd., Tom Greenwood at The Stroke Association, Lil Sullivan, Sandy
Halls at the Nightingale House Care Home and Burton's Food.

THE COMPANY

LUKE NORRIS (Writer)

Goodbye to All That, which is Luke's professional debut, was developed with The Royal Court through one of the Studio Playwriting Groups. He hopes to return to The Royal Court to be part of the Invitation Group later this year.

His play Borough Market was commissioned and produced for The Edinburgh Fringe Festival in 2008 by theatre company Breaking Butterflies. MacDonald and Son, his second play, was developed with Jane Fallowfield and Root Theatre and received a staged reading as part of Up Rooted at ATC.

Luke wrote the graduation film Sparks for the Directing Fiction course at the NFTS 2010 and is currently writing short film, Night of the Foxes, for Director Tom Haines.

Luke is also an actor; his recent credits include: Remembrance Day (Royal Court); The Kitchen & The Habit of Art (National Theatre); The Gods Weep, Days of Significance (RSC); War Horse (West End).

SUSAN BROWN (Iris)

FOR THE ROYAL COURT: Road, Shirley, Downfall, Gibraltar Strait, Seagulls.

OTHER THEATRE INCLUDES: Harper Regan, The Hour We Knew Nothing of Each Other, Playing With Fire, Henry IV Parts I & II, Cardiff East (National); Easter, Romeo & Juliet, Richard III, Bad Weather (RSC); Saved (Lyric Hammersmith); Dying For It, Butterfly Kiss (Almeida); The Wild Duck (Donmar); The Contingency Plan (Bush); The Chairs, The House of Bernarda Alba (Gate); You Be Ted and I'll Be Sylvia (Hampstead); The Beaux Stratagem, Back to Methuselah, The Vortex, The Way of the World, A Woman of No Importance (Cambridge Theatre Company); Playing Sinatra (Warehouse/Greenwich Theatre); Twelfth Night (English Touring Theatre); Small Change, Iphigenia (Sheffield Theatres).

TELEVISION INCLUDES: Stella, Midsomer Murders, Waking the Dead, Game of Thrones, Torchwood, Silent Witness, Blue Dove, Dalziel & Pascoe, Brides in the Bath, La Femme Musketeer, Rose & Maloney, Pinochet in Suburbia, Loving Hazel, Making Out, Coronation Street, Absolute Hell, Nona, Prime Suspect, The Riff Raff Element, September Song, A Touch of Frost, Taggart, Wokenwell, Anorak of Fire, The Vice, Wire in the Blood, The Best of Both Worlds, Road.

FILM INCLUDES: The Iron Lady, Now Is Good, Brideshead Revisited, Hope & Glory.

ALEXANDER CAPLEN (Sound Designer)

FOR THE ROYAL COURT: Wanderlust, Over There (& Schaubühne, Berlin).

OTHER THEATRE INCLUDES: The Golden Dragon (ATC); Ogres (Tristan Bates); It's About Time (Nabokov); The Love for Three Oranges, Tosca (Grange Park Opera); Mine, Ten Tiny Toes, War and Peace (Shared Experience); Stephen and the Sexy Partridge (Old Red Lion/ Trafalgar Studios); Peter Pan, Holes, Duck Variations (UK Tour); The Wizard of Oz, The Entertainer (Nuffield Theatre); Imogen (Oval House/Tour).

AS SOUND OPERATOR/ENGINEER CREDITS INCLUDE: Edinburgh Military Tattoo 2009 - 2011; Bronte, Kindertransport (Shared Experience UK Tour); Blood Brothers (International tour); Ballroom (UK tour). Other work includes large-scale international music touring as a Front of House mix engineer.

Alex is Sound Deputy at The Royal Court and an Associate Artist (Sound) for ATC.

ALEXANDER COBB (David)

THEATRE INCLUDES: Two Gentlemen of Verona (Royal & Derngate); Wasted (Paines Plough & Latitude).

TELEVISION INCLUDES: Parades End.

MATT DRURY (Lighting Designer)

FOR THE ROYAL COURT: Birth of a Nation, The Mother, Shades, The Stone, The Author (& UK Tour); Ingredient X, Over There (& Schaubühne, Berlin).

OTHER THEATRE INCLUDES: Private Lives, Same Time Next Year, Absent Friends, Absurd Person Singular, Deadly Nightcap, Bedroom Farce, Sweet Revenge, Joking Apart, Dead Certain, Cinderella, Dangerous Obsession, Spider's Web (Theatre Royal Windsor); Under Their Hats (Thorndike Theatre, Leatherhead, & West End); Nicholas Nickleby, The Hollow Crown, Guys and Dolls, (Thorndike Theatre, Leatherhead); The Flipside, Shirley Valentine, The Gentle Hook (Bill Kenwright); Fools Rush In (UK Tour); Funny Money (UK Tour); Two of A Kind (UK Tour); Catch Me If You Can (UK Tour); Framed (National); Cassie (Everyman, Cheltenham); Scooping the Pot (UK Tour); Daemons (European Tour); The Hollow (UK Tour), The Unexpected Guest (UK Tour); The Haunted Hotel (UK Tour); Arsenic and Old Lace (UK Tour) and An Ideal Husband (UK Tour).

SIMON GODWIN (Director)

FOR THE ROYAL COURT: The Acid Test, Pagans (International Playwrights Season 2011); Wanderlust, Hung Over: Ten Short Plays About The Election (Rough Cut); After the Spring (International Rough Cut); Black Beast Sadness (Off the Wall Season Reading); Hassan Lekliche (I Come From There Season Reading).

OTHER THEATRE INCLUDES: Faith Healer, Far Away (Bristol Old Vic); The Winter's Tale (Headlong with Nuffield Theatre and Schtanhaus, UK tour); All the Little Things We Crushed (Almeida Projects); The Country (Tabard); The Seagull, Habeas Corpus, Relatively Speaking (Royal & Derngate Theatres, Northampton); Quartermaine's Terms (Royal & Derngate Theatres with Salisbury Playhouse); Mister Heracles (West Yorkshire Playhouse); Romeo & Juliet (Cambridge Arts Theatre); All's Well That Ends Well (Straydogs/UK Tour); Eurydice (Straydogs, BAC/Trafalgar Studios).

OPERA INCLUDES: Inkle and Yarico (Straydogs).

RADIO INCLUDES: Chicken Soup with Barley.

Co-founder of Straydogs Theatre Company & Associate Director of the Royal & Derngate Theatres, Northampton (2001-2004).

Simon is currently an Associate Director of Bristol Old Vic and the Royal Court.

ALICE LACEY (Assistant Director)

AS ASSISTANT DIRECTOR FOR THE ROYAL COURT: Write Up There.

THEATRE DIRECTION INCLUDES: it is having fallen out of grace (Bush/Westminster Abbey); Recalculating, Soyuz-40 (Arcola); Limbs (Southwark Playhouse/Nabokov); Custard (OVNV), Fantasia (Old Vic 24 Hour Plays), After the Flood (Old Vic), The Ostrich and the Dolphin (Royal Institution/UK Tour).

OTHER ASSISTANT DIRECTION INCLUDES: Pericles (Regent's Park Open Air), Moonlight and Magnolias (Watermill), The Knowledge (Bush), Pencil (Old Vic Celebrity 24 Hour Plays), Moonfleece (UK Tour).

Alice is Artistic Director of Full Flight Theatre, Literary Associate for Angle Theatre and Co-Director of educational company now>press>play.

LINDA MARLOWE (Rita)

THEATRE INCLUDES: Decadence, The Trial, Metamorphosis, Hamlet, Greek, Coriolanus (West End); Too Clever By Half, A Flea in Her Ear (Old Vic); One Flew Over the Cuckoos Nest (Royal Exchange); A Streetcar Named Desire (Sherman Theatre, Cardiff); Callas (Oldham Coliseum); Suddenly Last Summer (Nottingham Playhouse); The Virtuoso, Twelfth Night, The Theban Trilogy (RSC); The Time Step (Edinburgh Fest.); Berkoff's Women, The World's Wife (International Tour/West End); Diatribe of Love, No Fear!, Mortal Ladies Possessed, Believe (UK/International Tour).

TV INCLUDES: Floodtide, The Avengers, The Queens Arms, The Fear, The Ruth Rendell Mysteries, The Green Man, Lovejoy, Love Hurts, Class Act, She's Out, Silent Witness, Dalziel & Pascoe, Midsomer Murders, Chambers, Family, Spooks, Foyle's War, I Shouldn't Be Alive, Jekyll.

FILM INCLUDES: Big Zapper, Beckett, The Man Outside, Tamlyn, Manifesto, Mr Love, The House of Mirth, Day of the Dead, Tinker Tailor Soldier Spy, The Wedding Video.

AS A DIRECTOR: Lunch (Library Theatre, Manchester/King's Head/New End/ Young Vic); Zoo Story (New End); Madhouse in Goa (Oldham Coliseum); Through the Leaves, A View From The Bridge, There Are Crimes And Crimes (Leicester Haymarket); Gala Dali (Old Red Lion); Invade My Privacy (Riverside); High Brave Boy (Edinburgh Fest.); Curry Tales, Shades of Brown (Library, Manchester/Edinburgh Fest.).

AWARDS INCLUDE: 1990 Manchester Evening News Award for Best Director, 2001 What's On Stage People's Choice Theatre Award for Best Actress for Berkoff's Women.

TOM PIPER (Designer)

THEATRE INCLUDES: Much Ado About Nothing, Macbeth, City Madam, Richard II, Henry IV – Parts I and II, Henry V, Henry VI – Parts I, II and III, Richard III, As You Like It, The Grain Store, The Drunks, Anthony and Cleopatra (RSC); Richard III, The Tempest, As You Like It (BAM & Old Vic); Zorro (West End, Paris, Moscow, Amsterdam, Tokyo); Dealer's Choice (Menier & West End); Falstaff (Scottish Opera); Fall (Traverse); Spyski (Lyric Hammersmith & Tour); The Scarecrow and His Servant (Southwark Playhouse); Plough and the Stars, The Crucible, Six Characters in Search of an Author (Abbey, Dublin).
AWARDS INCLUDE: 2009 Olivier Award for Best Costume Design for Richard III.
Tom is the Associate Designer at the RSC.

ROGER SLOMAN (Frank)

THEATRE INCLUDES: Mother Courage, Henry IV, The Mandate (National); Great Expectations, Much Ado About Nothing (RSC); The Faery Queen (Glyndebourne); The Iceman Cometh (Almeida); 2000 Feet Away (Bush); Henry V (Royal Exchange); Humble Boy (Northampton).
TELEVISION INCLUDES: Nuts in May, Small Island, Foyle's War, Midsomer Murders, Shameless, Vicar of Dibley, Mr Bean, Holby City.
FILM INCLUDES: Reds, Loch Ness, Young Indiana Jones, Beautiful People, Sorted, Beowulf.

THE ENGLISH STAGE COMPANY
AT THE ROYAL COURT THEATRE

'For me the theatre is really a religion or way of life. You must decide what you feel the world is about and what you want to say about it, so that everything in the theatre you work in is saying the same thing ... A theatre must have a recognisable attitude. It will have one, whether you like it or not.'

George Devine, first artistic director of the English Stage Company: notes for an unwritten book.

photo: Stephen Cummiskey

As Britain's leading national company dedicated to new work, the Royal Court Theatre produces new plays of the highest quality, working with writers from all backgrounds, and addressing the problems and possibilities of our time.

"The Royal Court has been at the centre of British cultural life for the past 50 years, an engine room for new writing and constantly transforming the theatrical culture." Stephen Daldry

Since its foundation in 1956, the Royal Court has presented premieres by almost every leading contemporary British playwright, from John Osborne's Look Back in Anger to Caryl Churchill's A Number and Tom Stoppard's Rock 'n' Roll. Just some of the other writers to have chosen the Royal Court to premiere their work include Edward Albee, John Arden, Richard Bean, Samuel Beckett, Edward Bond, Leo Butler, Jez Butterworth, Martin Crimp, Ariel Dorfman, Stella Feehily, Christopher Hampton, David Hare, Eugène Ionesco, Ann Jellicoe, Terry Johnson, Sarah Kane, David Mamet, Martin McDonagh, Conor McPherson, Joe Penhall, Lucy Prebble, Mark Ravenhill, Simon Stephens, Wole Soyinka, Polly Stenham, David Storey, Debbie Tucker Green, Arnold Wesker and Roy Williams.

"It is risky to miss a production there." Financial Times

In addition to its full-scale productions, the Royal Court also facilitates international work at a grass roots level, developing exchanges which bring young writers to Britain and sending British writers, actors and directors to work with artists around the world. The research and play development arm of the Royal Court Theatre, The Studio, finds the most exciting and diverse range of new voices in the UK. The Studio runs play-writing groups including the Young Writers Programme, Critical Mass for black, Asian and minority ethnic writers and the biennial Young Writers Festival. For further information, go to www.royalcourttheatre.com/playwriting/the-studio.

"Yes, the Royal Court is on a roll. Yes, Dominic Cooke has just the genius and kick that this venue needs... It's fist-bitingly exciting." Independent

ROYAL COURT SUPPORTERS

The Royal Court is able to offer its unique playwriting and audience development programmes because of significant and longstanding partnerships with the organisations that support it.

Coutts is the Principal Sponsor of the Royal Court. The Genesis Foundation supports the Royal Court's work with International Playwrights. Theatre Local is sponsored by Bloomberg. The Jerwood Charitable Foundation supports new plays by playwrights through the Jerwood New Playwrights series. Over the past ten years the BBC has supported the Gerald Chapman Fund for directors.

The Harold Pinter Playwright's Award is given annually by his widow, Lady Antonia Fraser, to support a new commission at the Royal Court.

PUBLIC FUNDING
Arts Council England, London
British Council
European Commission Representation in the UK

CHARITABLE DONATIONS
American Friends of the Royal Court
Martin Bowley Charitable Trust
Gerald Chapman Fund
City Bridge Trust
Cowley Charitable Trust
The H and G de Freitas Charitable Trust
The Dorset Foundation
The John Ellerman Foundation
The Eranda Foundation
Genesis Foundation
J Paul Getty Jnr Charitable Trust
The Golden Bottle Trust
The Haberdashers' Company
Paul Hamlyn Foundation
Jerwood Charitable Foundation
Marina Kleinwort Charitable Trust
The Leathersellers' Company
John Lyon's Charity
The Andrew W Mellon Foundation
The David & Elaine Potter Foundation
Rose Foundation
Royal Victoria Hall Foundation
The Dr Mortimer & Theresa Sackler Foundation
The Steel Charitable Trust
John Thaw Foundation
The Garfield Weston Foundation

CORPORATE SUPPORTERS & SPONSORS
BBC
Bloomberg
Coutts
Ecosse Films
Grey London
Kudos Film & Television
MAC
Moët & Chandon
Oakley Capital Limited
Sky Arts
Smythson of Bond Street
White Light Ltd

BUSINESS ASSOCIATES, MEMBERS & BENEFACTORS
Auerbach & Steele Opticians
Bank of America Merrill Lynch
Hugo Boss
Lazard
Louis Vuitton
Oberon Books
Peter Jones
Savills
Vanity Fair

DEVELOPMENT ADVOCATES
John Ayton MBE
Elizabeth Bandeen
Kinvara Balfour
Anthony Burton CBE
Piers Butler
Sindy Caplan
Sarah Chappatte
Cas Donald (Vice Chair)
Allie Esiri
Celeste Fenichel
Emma Marsh (Chair)
William Russell
Deborah Shaw Marquardt (Vice Chair)
Sian Westerman
Nick Wheeler
Daniel Winterfeldt

Supported by
ARTS COUNCIL ENGLAND

INDIVIDUAL MEMBERS

ICE-BREAKERS
ACT IV
Anonymous
Mrs Rosemary Alexander
Tony & Gabriela Ball
Kinvara Balfour
David Barnes
Lisa & Andrew Barnett
Mrs Renate Blackwood
Ossi & Paul Burger
Helena Butler
Leigh & Lena Collins
Mr Claes Hesselgren & Mrs Jane Collins
Mark & Tobey Dichter
Ms P Dolphin
Sally England
Elizabeth & James Downing
Virginia Finegold
Charlotte & Nick Fraser
Alistair & Lynwen Gibbons
Mr & Mrs Green
Sebastian & Rachel Grigg
Mrs Hattrell
Madeleine Hodgkin
Cindy Holmes
Steven & Candice Hurwitz
Mrs R Jay
David Lanch
Louisa Lane Fox
Yasmine Lever
Colette & Peter Levy
Mr & Mrs Peter Lord
David Marks QC
Nicola McFarland
Mr & Mrs Alex Nourry
Emma O'Donoghue
Michael & Janet Orr
Mrs Barbara Poeton
Really Useful Theatres
Mr & Mrs Tim Reid
Mrs Lois Sieff OBE
Mr & Mrs L Slaughter
Nick & Louise Steidl
Torsten Thiele
Susan & Graham White
Louise & Stephen Wisking
Laura & Stephen Zimmerman

GROUND-BREAKERS
Anonymous
Moira Andreae
Simon Andrews
Nick Archdale
Charlotte Asprey
Jane Attias
Caroline Baker
Brian Balfour-Oatts
Elizabeth & Adam Bandeen
Ray Barrell
Dr Kate Best
Dianne & Michael Bienes
Stan & Val Bond
Kristina Borsy & Nick Turdean
Neil & Sarah Brener
Mrs Deborah Brett
Sindy & Jonathan Caplan
Gavin & Lesley Casey
Sarah & Philippe Chappatte
Christine Collins
Tim & Caroline Clark
Carole & Neville Conrad
Kay Ellen Consolver & John Storkerson
Anthony & Andrea Coombs
Clyde Cooper
Ian & Caroline Cormack
Mr & Mrs Cross
Andrew & Amanda Cryer
Alison Davies
Noel De Keyzer
Polly Devlin OBE
Glen Donovan
Rob & Cherry Dickins
Denise & Randolph Dumas
Zeina Durra & Saadi Soudavar
Robyn Durie
Glenn & Phyllida Earle
Allie Esiri
Mark & Sarah Evans
Margaret Exley CBE
Celeste & Peter Fenichel
Margy Fenwick
John Garfield
Beverley Gee
Dina Geha & Eric Lopez
Mr & Mrs Georgiades
Nick & Julie Gould
Lord & Lady Grabiner
Richard & Marcia Grand
Reade & Elizabeth Griffith
Don & Sue Guiney
Jill Hackel & Andrzej Zarzycki
Carol Hall
Mary & Douglas Hampson
Sally Hampton
Jennifer Harper
Sam & Caroline Haubold
Anoushka Healy
Mr & Mrs Johnny Hewett
Gordon Holmes
Damien Hyland
The David Hyman Charitable Trust
Nicholas Jones
Nicholas Josefowitz
Dr Evi Kaplanis
David Kaskel & Christopher Teano
Vincent & Amanda Keaveny
Peter & Maria Kellner
Nicola Kerr
Diala & Tarek Khlat
Philip & Joan Kingsley
Mr & Mrs Pawel Kisielewski
Sarah & David Kowitz
Maria Lam
Larry & Peggy Levy
Daisy & Richard Littler
Kathryn Ludlow
James & Beatrice Lupton
Dr Ekaterina Malievskaia & George Goldsmith
Christopher Marek Rencki
Barbara Minto
Ann & Gavin Neath CBE
Murray North
Clive & Annie Norton
Georgia Oetker
William Plapinger & Cassie Murray
Andrea & Hilary Ponti
Annie & Preben Prebensen
Julie Ritter
Mark & Tricia Robinson
Paul & Gill Robinson
William & Hilary Russell
Julie & Bill Ryan
Sally & Anthony Salz
Bhags Sharma
Mrs Doris Sherwood
The Michael & Melanie Sherwood Charitable Foundation
Tom Siebens & Mimi Parsons
Andy Simpkin
Richard Simpson
Paul & Rita Skinner
Mr & Mrs Rah Smart
Brian Smith
Samantha & Darren Smith
Mr Michael Spencer
The Ulrich Family
The Ury Trust
Amanda Vail
Constance Von Unruh
Ian & Victoria Watson
Matthew & Sian Westerman
Carol Woolton
Katherine & Michael Yates

BOUNDARY-BREAKERS
Katie Bradford
Sir Trevor & Lady Chinn
Leonie Fallstrom
Piers & Melanie Gibson
Mr & Mrs Roderick Jack
Ms Alex Joffe
Steve Kingshott
Emma Marsh
Paul & Jill Ruddock
Mr & Mrs Nick Wheeler

MOVER-SHAKERS
Anonymous
Mr & Mrs Ayton MBE
Cas Donald
Lloyd & Sarah Dorfman
Lydia & Manfred Gorvy
Duncan Matthews QC
Ian & Carol Sellars
Edgar & Judith Wallner

HISTORY-MAKERS
Eric Abraham & Sigrid Rausing

MAJOR DONORS
Rob & Siri Cope
Daniel & Joanna Friel
Jack & Linda Keenan
Deborah & Stephen Marquardt
Miles Morland
Lady Sainsbury of Turville
NoraLee & Jon Sedmak
Jan & Michael Topham
Stuart & Hilary Williams Charitable Foundation

young writers festival 2012

Debut plays from young British playwrights with original and diverse stories to tell.

Since 1973, the Young Writers Festival has been unrivalled in its discovery of new writing, launching writers such as **Bola Agbaje, Alia Bano, Leo Butler, Andrea Dunbar, DC Moore, Chloe Moss, Christopher Shinn, Simon Stephens** and **Michael Wynne.**

22 March – 14 April
vera vera vera
by Hayley Squires

A bracing new voice, clear eyed and loud, looking at violence, neglect and apathy.

March – April
festival readings

Four play readings by writers aged 18–25.

17 March
saturday shorts

Play readings by writers aged 8–15.

1 & 14 & 29 March
in conversation

with the writers **Luke Norris** and **Hayley Squires** and designers **Ultz** and **Tom Piper**.

16, 28 Mar & 14 Apr
afterdark

Late night series of spoken word, music and a literary ball.

100 word play

Writers of all ages and experiences are invited to write us a play, to be displayed in and around the building.
royalcourttheatre.com/ 100wordplay

www.royalcourttheatre.com/ywf2012

The Young Writers Festival is supported by the National Lottery through Arts Council England and is in partnership with the European Commission Representation in the UK, with additional support from the Dr. Mortimer and Theresa Sackler Foundation.

The Young Writers Festival Development Phase has been supported by John Lyon's Charity.

Principal Sponsor

GOODBYE TO ALL THAT

Luke Norris

For C.T. Fancourt

Acknowledgements

Thanks to Leo Butler, Clare McQuillan and all involved with the Royal Court Studio Group and YWF.

Thanks to Romford Golf Club, Nightingale House, and my nan for their help and hospitality in researching the play.

Thanks to Samuel Adamson and Tessa Walker for, all those moons ago, letting me believe I had something worth pursuing in the first place.

Thanks to the cast of *Goodbye…* for their commitment and enthusiasm, and to Simon for his superhuman patience.

Most of all, thanks to Jo – without whom this play just wouldn't have been written. Thank you. And sorry for being a pain in the arse.

Luke Norris

'Please release me, let me go,
For I don't love you any more,
To waste our lives would be a sin,
Release me, and let me love again.'

Eddie Miller, 1946

Characters

DAVID, *eighteen*
FRANK, *sixty-nine*
RITA, *sixties*
IRIS, *sixties*

A forward slash (/) in the text indicates the point at which the next speaker interrupts.

Square brackets [ ] indicate a word or part of a word implied but not spoken.

This text went to press before the end of rehearsals and so may differ slightly from the play as performed.

PART ONE

One

A golf-club lounge-bar, afternoon.

DAVID, *eighteen, in the remnants of his school uniform, sitting in an armchair. He has two drinks in front of him.*

FRANK, *sixty-nine, has just entered.*

FRANK. David.

DAVID. Hello.

FRANK. You're in my chair. What are you doing here?

DAVID. Two A's / and a C…

FRANK. You should've phoned.

DAVID. Thanks for asking.

FRANK. What?

DAVID. Two A's and a C.

FRANK. It's today. Course it is. How'd you go?

DAVID. Guess.

FRANK. Well that's… Will that do it?

DAVID. No.

FRANK. Oh.

DAVID. It won't.

FRANK. Well.

Beat.

What was the C?

DAVID. Psychology.

FRANK. Psychology. So what does that mean?

DAVID. Leicester.

FRANK. Leicester, well. Castle. Cathedral.

Beat.

National Gas Museum.

Beat.

I'll drink to that.

DAVID. I got you one.

He holds it out.

Bell's. Bottled Coke and one piece of ice in a bowl glass.

FRANK. Who served you?

DAVID. The fat woman.

FRANK. Brenda?

DAVID. Moustache.

FRANK. Jeanie.

DAVID. Maybe.

FRANK. Unfortunate. The women call her Poirot.

DAVID. What?

FRANK. The lady golfers. She used to shave it. Or wax it.
    Now…

DAVID. Nice.

FRANK. I shall have to have words. Serving you.

DAVID. I am old enough.

FRANK. You're not a member.

DAVID. She knew it was for you when I asked.

FRANK *smiles*.

FRANK. Course she did. Well then.

   He charges his glass.

   Here's to you.

   DAVID *picks up his drink.*

   And what's in store.

   FRANK *drinks*. DAVID *downs half of his and winces.*

   What's in there?

DAVID. Orange.

FRANK. And?

DAVID. Vodka.

FRANK. Here.

DAVID. What for?

FRANK. I want to smell it.

DAVID. I've just told you what it is.

FRANK. I'm checking it's a single.

DAVID. It's not.

FRANK. Well. Go easy. It's early.

   He charges his glass again.

   And don't tell your grandma.

DAVID. She said you were playing golf with Mike Holdsworth.

FRANK. Hmm?

DAVID. Nan – I phoned home – she said you were here with
   Mike / Holdsworth.

FRANK. Oh. Yeah. Yes.

DAVID. Yeah?

FRANK. Just finished.

DAVID. Early.

FRANK. Eh?

DAVID. Like you said. It's early.

FRANK. The weather.

DAVID. Right.

FRANK. Had enough.

DAVID. Have you. Where is he?

FRANK. Who?

DAVID. Mike Holdsworth.

FRANK. Oh. Gone. Went straight off.

DAVID. Did he.

FRANK. Shot a stinker. Copped the hump.

DAVID. Shame.

FRANK. Well. I owed him one.

   DAVID *downs the rest of his drink.*

DAVID. Same again?

FRANK. Something the matter, son?

DAVID. Why would there be?

FRANK. Well.

DAVID. I like the taste.

FRANK. It's two o' clock.

DAVID. I'm celebrating.

FRANK. With the best will in the world, son, you're going to Leicester.

   Beat.

DAVID. You know his grandson's in my form at school?

FRANK. Whose is?

DAVID. Billy.

FRANK. Holdsworth?

DAVID. His name's Billy, yeah – he couldn't get there today. For the results. He's thick as shit anyway / but…

FRANK. Oi.

DAVID.…he's in Gran Canaria with his parents.

FRANK. Well. Alright for some.

DAVID. Yeah. The hotel's got a bar in the swimming pool, apparently.

FRANK. A bar in the swimming pool, / eh?

DAVID. Guess who they sent to get his grades instead?

Beat.

He looked like a right prick doddering around the school on his own. He'd managed to get lost, ended up by the boys' toilets. If I didn't know better I'd say he was dodgy – with his gold tooth, and his rain mac. And his wig.

Beat.

No? I'll give you another clue: he wasn't here and he wasn't losing a round of golf to you.

Beat.

Who's she?

FRANK. Who?

DAVID. The woman you just played golf with.

Beat.

The one you were holding hands with. The one you patted on the arse as she got in her big flash car.

FRANK. No one.

DAVID. Oh.

FRANK. A friend.

DAVID. Do you think I'm stupid?

FRANK. No.

DAVID. Because I'm not / stupid.

FRANK. No.

DAVID. No. So?

Beat.

Shame she didn't come in. I had a vodka and orange waiting for her. Treble. What's her name?

FRANK. David…

DAVID. Funny name for an old slapper.

FRANK. Her name's Rita.

DAVID. And?

FRANK. And what?

DAVID. What's the deal?

FRANK. 'The deal'?

DAVID. Do you love her?

FRANK. Look, / son…

DAVID. 'Cause it's not sex, is it. Do you love Nan?

FRANK. Listen to me…

DAVID. Go on then.

FRANK. It's not as simple as that.

DAVID. Why not?

FRANK. Because it's not.

DAVID. Seems pretty simple to me; you either love her / or you don't.

FRANK. Yes, well, you'll understand one day.

DAVID. When I'm older?

FRANK. Exactly.

DAVID. Fuck off.

Beat.

FRANK. You watch your mouth when you speak to me.

DAVID. Or what? You'll tell my nan?

Beat.

You know I always thought, whatever you were... and I'm not saying, y'know... but I thought you were decent. A decent man. Shows what I know.

Beat.

Your round.

FRANK. Does your grandma know you've come here?

Beat.

Does she, David?

DAVID. No.

FRANK. Good. Good, now listen to me –

DAVID. Leave her. Your girlfriend. Whatever she is, leave her today. Now.

FRANK. Leaving her isn't / going to...

DAVID. Do it or I'll tell Nan and I'll pack your bags myself. Then you can come down here and pat your girlfriend's wrinkled old arse 'til you both drop down dead.

Beat.

Up to you, old man. What's more important?

Two

RITA*'s living room, late afternoon / early evening.*

FRANK *in an outdoor coat, soaking wet.*

RITA, *sixties, half-dressed for dinner.*

RITA. You're wet. You're drenched, you're… you're soaked through. Why are / you…?

FRANK. I walked.

RITA. From the golf club? It's miles.

FRANK. It's not that far.

RITA. It's teeming down. I would have driven you if I'd / known.

FRANK. I wanted the walk.

RITA. In this? You look as though you swam here.

She smiles. He doesn't.

Are you…?

FRANK. I'm fine. Could do with a drink.

RITA. Do you want to take your coat off?

FRANK. No. Yes. I do.

He doesn't take his coat off.

RITA. Are you sure you're alright?

FRANK. Yeah. Yes, / I'm…

RITA. Because you're being a bit…

FRANK. I know.

RITA. I wasn't expecting you.

FRANK. When?

RITA. Now. Here. I thought we were meeting at the restaurant.

FRANK. Oh…

RITA. You won't have to wear that to dinner?

FRANK. No.

RITA. I don't think you've got anything / here.

FRANK. I'm not coming.

RITA. You're…?

FRANK. Not coming. To dinner.

RITA. Oh. I see.

Beat.

Why not?

Beat.

It doesn't have to be Italian.

FRANK. What do you think of me, Chuck?

RITA. Sorry?

Beat.

What do I *think* / of you?

FRANK. Am I a good man?

RITA. A – what? Of course you are.

FRANK. Am I?

RITA. Yes.

FRANK. Decent? / Am I?

RITA. Yes, you're… Yes, you are.

FRANK. I don't think I am. And I don't think I care any more.

RITA. Frankie… what are you talking about?

FRANK. The boy. He knows.

RITA. David?

FRANK. Yeah.

RITA. He knows what? What does he know?

He just looks at her.

Beat.

Oh.

FRANK. Yeah.

RITA. I see.

FRANK. I can't…

RITA. How?

FRANK. The relief / is…

RITA. How does – ? Relief?

FRANK. Relief, yeah. Yes, relief; I'm sick of it. I am sick to the marrow of pretending. Pretending to be this… this…

RITA. What?

FRANK. I want to do what I *want*, Chuck – I always have done, since I was a boy – and instead I've spent the best part of my life…

RITA. Pretending.

FRANK. Pretending. Exactly. And why? For what?

RITA. For, well, for… for your family.

FRANK. My family?

RITA. Yes. For David, and…

Beat.

FRANK. And?

RITA. And Iris.

FRANK. Iris. / Yeah.

RITA. I'd say – yes – whatever you think, I'd say that makes you good.

FRANK. I go to bed at night and I wish it'd never happened. I lay there in those same sheets night on night and I curse the day I met her.

RITA. You don't mean that.

FRANK. I do.

RITA. No. No, without her there'd have been no Barbara...

FRANK. Well, look how / that turned out.

RITA. And without Barbara there would be no David. So.

FRANK. I – honest to God – I sometimes wish there wasn't.

RITA. Frankie.

FRANK. Now you tell me: what's so good about that? Where's the *good* in that, Chuck?

RITA. I don't know.

FRANK. No. Nor do I. But that's what they'll say, when it's all over: 'He was good. A good man. A decent man.' Because they don't know. Because I never had the nerve to do what I wanted.

RITA. How many people do? Really?

FRANK. You did.

RITA. No...

FRANK. No?

RITA. Or it's nothing to do with nerve... I got lucky.

FRANK. Lucky.

RITA. Very.

FRANK. So. What does that make me?

RITA. Things haven't been so bad for you either, Frankie. Not in the grand scheme.

FRANK. I don't get to live the grand scheme, do I? I get my life. One. And I've wasted it.

RITA. Making other people happy isn't a waste of a life.

FRANK. Who am I making happy, Chuck?

RITA. Me, for one.

FRANK. Not really.

RITA. Yes.

FRANK. Not *really*, and I should be. I should, I – these should be the bloody 'bar in the swimming pool' years, shouldn't they?

RITA. The / what?

FRANK. We should be sipping margaritas on a lilo somewhere. Off in the sun, just us.

RITA. That sounds nice.

FRANK. Instead – here we are.

RITA. Yes here we are.

FRANK. Here we both are. Do you love me, Chuck?

Beat.

RITA. Sorry?

FRANK. Do you love me?

RITA. Frankie… How much have you had / to drink?

FRANK. Chuck. Do you?

Beat. They look at each other.

RITA. Yes, I do, I suppose I do.

FRANK. Thank you.

Beat.

'What's more important?' he says to me.

Beat.

I'm not coming to dinner, Chuck. I'm going home to leave my wife.

Three

IRIS *and* FRANK*'s hallway, early evening. A telephone on a table.*

FRANK, *as before, and* IRIS, *sixties, in her slippers.*

IRIS. W – ?

They look at each other.

What?

Beat.

I don't…

FRANK *nods. Looks at his feet.*

But it's a Thursday, I'm making stew. I've got… I've got a stew on.

FRANK. Yeah.

Beat.

Look…

IRIS. Why?

He just looks at her.

Frank.

FRANK. You know why.

IRIS. No I – no, I – don't tell me what I know. Why?

Beat.

Frank!

FRANK. I don't love you.

IRIS. 'Love'? [You] talk about 'love'? We've… we're, we're, we're, we've got a *life*. We've got a *life* – we've *given* – there's people *exist* because of us, / you talk about 'love'?

FRANK. Not people. Not any more.

IRIS. You've thought about David, have you?

FRANK. Of course I / have.

IRIS. How he's going to react to all this?

FRANK. He'll be fine.

IRIS. Will he now?

FRANK. He's got his head screwed on.

IRIS. And what about you? Have you got yours on, have you?

FRANK. Yes. I have. For the first time / in...

IRIS. No no no no no!

FRANK. We're not happy, I [ris]. Are we?

IRIS. Happy?

FRANK. Neither of us. Why spend the rest of our lives pretending we are?

IRIS. Because! Because we're married and that's what you do.

FRANK. Why?

IRIS. Bec– forty-five years we've been married.

FRANK. I know how long we've / been...

IRIS. Forty-five years – a lifetime. 'The rest of our lives'? Our lives are bleedin' – we've had our lives. This is it. This is what we did with them.

FRANK. Well I'm not prepared to settle for that.

IRIS. Tough. Hard luck; you're too old for anything else. We both are; we're too old to, to, to – look at you. Settle? You cheeky... This is stupid. What are you going to do? What am I? It's silly, it's stupid, it's bloody – you've been drinking is what it is.

FRANK. No.

IRIS. You and what's-his-name...

FRANK. Iris.

IRIS. Mickey, bleedin'…

FRANK. Iris.

IRIS. Mike Holdsworth.

FRANK. No!

IRIS. You've gone and had a skinful and he's / put ideas…

FRANK. I wasn't with him, I [ris].

IRIS. He's put this into your head.

FRANK. I haven't been with Holdsworth! I haven't played golf
    with him for nine months? A year? I haven't *seen* him since
    Christmas. I've been with a woman, Iris.

IRIS. You've…?

FRANK. Yeah, I've… Yes. I have.

    Beat.

IRIS. So that's it – I mean, that's *it*: 'I'm not prepared to settle'?
    Rubbish! It's because you've got a tart. Who is it?

    Beat.

    How long's it been going / on?

FRANK. Iris.

IRIS. Who is she?!

    Beat.

FRANK. Rita. Berry.

IRIS. Berry.

    Beat.

    She was married to that fella from the club.

FRANK. Harry.

IRIS. Harry Berry. Had cancer, they had to cut half his face
    away. We went to the funeral.

FRANK. He's been dead a long time.

IRIS. I'm not dead, am I?! Am I?

Beat.

You…

IRIS *is trembling.*

I was doing you a party. For your seventieth. I'm doing you a party at the club, I spoke to what's-her-name, the barmaid with the face… I've booked The Burns Brothers. I've booked The Burns Brothers – they had to cancel another do – what am I supposed to tell them?

FRANK *shakes his head. Shrugs.*

FRANK. Tell them what you like, I [ris].

IRIS. Will she do you a party, this woman? This 'Rita'?

Beat.

FRANK. I hope not.

IRIS. You… You f…

It is all IRIS *can do to hold herself together.*

Beat.

FRANK. I'll get some bits.

IRIS. No you won't, I'll do you a case – you can come back and get it.

FRANK. If that's what you want.

IRIS. And you're out of the way before David gets back in the morning, you hear?

FRANK. I'm sorry, I [ris].

IRIS. Are you? I'm not.

FRANK. In some ways.

IRIS. Well… now you feel better you can go on and fuck off.

Four

The golf club. Evening.

FRANK *is in his armchair. On the table in front of him is his drink the way he takes it, and his mobile phone.*

DAVID, *standing.*

DAVID. Are you still here?

FRANK. Pinch me.

DAVID. What?

FRANK. Pinch me. Find out.

> *Beat.*

DAVID. You're drunk.

FRANK. Am I?

DAVID. Have you even moved?

FRANK. Look at me moving. I'm expert at it.

DAVID. What are you doing?

FRANK. What happened to your party, David? You were going out.

DAVID. You were going home.

FRANK. 'House party', you / said.

DAVID. I phoned. Nan said she hadn't seen you.

FRANK. Did she.

DAVID. You should've been there by now. What happened?

FRANK. You the police?

DAVID. Granddad.

FRANK. Because if you're the police you're not doing a very good / job.

DAVID. What are you doing here?

FRANK. I'm having a drink. What are you doing here?

DAVID. Looking for you.

FRANK. Well. Ta-da.

DAVID. Have you done it?

FRANK. Go back to your do, David.

DAVID. Have you spoken to / that woman?

FRANK. Go back to your sleepover – it'll be more fun.

DAVID. You think I want to be standing here doing this?

FRANK. Then why are you? Eh? Why are you standing here? No one's asked you to come, have they?

Beat.

No.

DAVID. You don't even care, do you?

FRANK. Oh, I care, son.

DAVID. Then do the right thing.

FRANK. I already have.

Beat.

DAVID. Yeah?

FRANK. What time is it?

DAVID. You've done it?

FRANK. You want one?

DAVID. Granddad.

FRANK. Vodka and orange, / isn't it?

DAVID. Have you left her?

FRANK. Poof's drink, that…

DAVID. Answer me.

FRANK. Careful. People'll / talk.

DAVID. Granddad. Have you done it?

FRANK. Oh, I've done it, son. I've really done it.

Beat.

She blames me for your mother, you know. Never said so,
but…

DAVID. What?

FRANK. Your grandma. She blames me.

DAVID. I don't wanna know.

FRANK. We never talked to you about her. Your mother. Your
grandma's idea, I'm sorry about that.

DAVID. I'm not.

FRANK. You would be. If you'd known her.

DAVID. I doubt it.

FRANK. You're not a bit like her. So serious.

DAVID. Good.

FRANK. But then you would be. Not so much to smile about /
since.

DAVID. Stop it.

FRANK. She helped you breathe, somehow.

DAVID. Granddad.

FRANK. She was light, you know.

DAVID. I / said –

FRANK. Lightness.

DAVID. Shut up!

FRANK. You don't tell me what to do!

Beat.

DAVID. She wasn't.

FRANK. You don't know what she was or / wasn't.

DAVID. She was weak.

FRANK. No.

DAVID. Otherwise she'd have been here, wouldn't she?

FRANK. Do you feel like an adult, David? You look in the mirror, do you see an adult? / A grown-up?

DAVID. Of course I do.

FRANK. I don't. The older you get the more you realise: you don't grow up. Not really. You just get older. And it is petrifying. Look at me – I'm every bit as scared as you are.

DAVID. I'm not scared.

FRANK. Yes you are. And if you're not, you bloody well should be.

Beat.

I could've gone to university. I'll bet you never knew that. Went to the market instead – my dad: 'What do you want to do that for?' I met your grandma… and now, here we are.

FRANK*'s phone starts ringing.*

Funny how things turn out, isn't it?

DAVID. Yeah. Hilarious.

FRANK *looks at the display on his phone.*

Is that Nan?

He turns the display to face DAVID.

Who's that? Who's Chuck?

FRANK *stands, groggily, to make his way out.*

FRANK. No phones in the clubhouse.

DAVID. Where are you going?

FRANK. To answer it.

DAVID snatches the phone from his hand. Beat.

Here.

DAVID. No.

FRANK. Give it to me.

The phone continues to ring. Beat.

DAVID answers it, his eyes locked on FRANK.

DAVID. Hello?

A second and he hangs up. He looks at the phone in his hand, looks to his granddad, then hurls it at the ground, smashing it to pieces.

Beat. FRANK grits his teeth.

FRANK. I want you to remember something, David –

DAVID. No, you can stop trying to / dish out…

FRANK. You listen to me, boy! Listen now: if you remember only one thing I've ever told you, you remember this every day, *every day* – morning, noon and night – you do what you want with your life. Alright? Exactly what you want. You break heads if you need to and hearts if you have to but you make sure, make *sure,* boy, that you find yourself love somewhere along the way. I mean it. Love. Love, love, love; don't settle for anything else – and once you've got it, hold onto it like a pitbull. Fight tooth and nail. Tell her every day and spend all the time you can surrounding yourself with it because believe you me, anything less is a waste of time. Whatever you do, don't do what I did.

Beat.

Don't waste yourself.

They look at each other a moment.

And FRANK exits, leaving DAVID alone.

Five

RITA*'s living room. Evening.*

FRANK *and* RITA *dancing.*

The music is old-fashioned: 'Illusion' by Nat King Cole, perhaps.

The dance, too, is old-fashioned.

Slow, romantic, happy.

As the dance continues, it becomes more expansive, more comfortable.

They warm into it, led by FRANK *who has had a drink or two.*

As they perform a turn, FRANK *gets his feet caught and falters.*

He quickly rights himself. A moment.

The pair look at each other.

They dissolve into laughter and return to a close embrace, swaying to the music.

FRANK*'s laughter dies away, his face clouding over slightly.*

RITA. I thought I'd lost you there for a moment.

They continue to sway almost imperceptibly now.

FRANK. Chuck.

Beat.

RITA. Mmm?

A long silence.

FRANK. Nothing.

Six

IRIS *and* FRANK*'s hallway, night.*

FRANK *seems drunk.* IRIS *has a suitcase at her feet.*

IRIS. You're wet. / All…

FRANK. I'm…

IRIS. Eh?

FRANK. Mmm.

IRIS. You've wet yourself.

FRANK. No.

IRIS. You have.

FRANK. Yeah.

IRIS. Why've you done that?

   Beat.

FRANK. Yeah.

IRIS. Eh? Why've you done that, you…?

   He just looks at her.

   Frank.

FRANK. I'm… / I'm…

IRIS. Go and – go on, clean yourself up, look. All wet, bleedin'
   – fancy standing there like that, silly sod, take them off;
   you'll be all – you'll start to smell you leave them on.

FRANK. Yeah.

IRIS. Frank.

   Beat.

   Well, go on then, get yourself some clean knickers on.

She edges the suitcase towards him.

He looks down at it and slowly starts unbuttoning his shirt.

What you doing that for? You old pisshead – hang on…

She kneels and lays down the suitcase, opening it up. Inside is a selection of FRANK's clothes, which she paws through for underwear.

…Bleedin' nuisance. You're lucky I'm…

FRANK *continues with the buttons on his shirt. His hands can't negotiate the task properly but he carries on, seemingly undeterred.*

IRIS *recovers some fresh underwear from the case.*

Here, look. Now sort yourself out.

She dangles the briefs out to him. He takes them, gently, and just holds them.

Beat.

What's the matter with you? Coming back like – you bloody come here in this state.

With effort, he manages –

FRANK. I'm…

IRIS. What?

FRANK *drops the briefs in his hands.* IRIS *picks them up again, stands and holds them out to him. He stares back glassily. She studies his face.*

What's…?

He gropes for speech.

What's the matter with you?

No response from FRANK, *who stays rooted to the spot, staring at her.*

Frank.

Beat.

She slaps him across the face. He winces and moves his hand towards his face… but that's all. She continues to look at him.

Well.

She briefly rubs the cheek she just slapped.

Let's get you sorted then.

She kneels on the floor at his feet, undoes his belt, and pulls down his trousers and his underpants – putting them all in a soggy pile away from her.

Come on then.

She holds out the clean briefs by his ankles.

Step.

He tentatively puts his hands on her shoulders and lifts one leg. She fishes his foot through the briefs and he puts it down again.

And the other one.

He falters once then lifts his other leg.

You… Playing silly buggers.

She hooks the pants around this ankle and yanks them up to his waist then picks pyjama trousers from the suitcase.

Again, then.

He lifts a foot, she feeds it through the trouser leg, he puts it down.

Other one.

They repeat the action the other side and she stands, pulling his trousers up.

You bleedin' piss-artist.

She undoes the rest of the buttons on his shirt and slides his shirt and coat off, during:

It's a wonder you don't do it every week, the state you come home in. It's that Mickey Hollingsworth. Holdsworth. Him and his money. The pair of you. Like bleedin' teenagers, the way you carry on.

She picks up his pyjama shirt and begins to put it on him.

I'd be embarrassed, it was me. Supposed to be there to play golf, not bloody – and you come home like this? Lucky. Intcha? Lucky for you I've got the patience of a saint. Eh? Lucky Frank. There then, you can finish yourself off. I'll go and…

She picks up the pile of damp clothes.

Buttons. Go on.

IRIS *goes off to the kitchen as* FRANK *begins to try and fasten the rest of his buttons. Again, it is slow, slow going.*

IRIS *returns, empty handed, and finishes off his buttons. She looks at him. Looks at the case.*

We'll leave that 'til the morning, shall we?

FRANK *just looks at her.*

We'll leave it for now.

Beat.

I've put clean sheets on.

She exits to the bedroom.

He stands there, unmoving. Looks down at his hand as if perhaps waiting for something.

His lips move.

He looks off, to the bedroom. Might be about to say something when darkness spreads down his leg from the crotch of his pyjamas.

He has wet himself again.

He looks down at himself and begins to silently cry.

Seven

A hospital waiting area, morning.

DAVID *standing,* IRIS *sitting.*

A bag of personal effects.

DAVID. Why didn't you phone me?

IRIS. I did phone you.

DAVID. Last night.

IRIS. Well, you were out, you were staying at your little
friend's, / celebrating.

DAVID. Someone else, then.

IRIS. Who?

DAVID. Anyone!

IRIS. You don't just go around phoning people in the middle of
the night.

DAVID. What?!

IRIS. You don't.

DAVID. What are you talking / about?!

IRIS. You don't go phoning people up in the night; you don't,
not unless somebody's died.

DAVID. He could have!

IRIS. Don't be dramatic.

DAVID. Nan, he's in intensive / care!

IRIS. I know where he is, thank you very much, and you can
keep your voice down as well. Make a bloody scene. He'll
be fine. It'll be a what-do-you-call-it… a prevention.

DAVID. A precaution.

IRIS. A – yes. That.

DAVID. And what if it's not?

Beat.

Nan.

IRIS. Then we'll see.

DAVID. Why didn't you phone an ambulance?

Beat.

Nan. Why didn't / you phone…

IRIS. Because I didn't know, did I? Alright? I don't know, do I? How am I supposed to know?

DAVID. The, the adverts, the… face, arms…

IRIS. I don't watch the television.

DAVID. You do. They're on bus stops / and…

IRIS. Well, excuse me, I'm sorry, I don't get the bus either.

DAVID. Face, arms, speech…

IRIS. I don't know what you're talking / about.

DAVID. FAST. The quicker you catch it, the more they can do.

IRIS. No, that's – they can't, they've said.

DAVID. Said what?

IRIS. They've said it can take over two days for it to, to what's-it, to complete so it doesn't make the blindest bit of difference.

DAVID. But they'll have been able to do something about it, / if…

IRIS. No, they don't, they leave it, I asked the woman. They might have give him a paracetamol, she said – if you live up town or somewhere there's a drug but they don't give it in Romford, so that's / that, you…

DAVID. Why not? Why don't they give it here?

IRIS. Well, I don't know, do I? It'll be the health authority, or –
anyway, that's it; you see it out – so don't give me this
business about how if I'd got him here in five minutes he'd
be turning / cartwheels.

DAVID. I'm not saying… it's not like I'm saying it's your fault,
I'm…

IRIS. Right, yes, well then, what are you saying?

DAVID. I'm… Nothing.

IRIS. Good.

Beat.

DAVID. When was the last time you spoke to anyone?

IRIS. Oh, I don't know, two hours ago.

DAVID. And?

IRIS. They wouldn't tell me.

DAVID. I'm gonna go and find someone.

IRIS. You stay where you are. Last thing they need is you
sticking your oar in – sit yourself down, go on.

DAVID. What's that?

IRIS. His things.

DAVID. What things?

IRIS. His bedclothes, his slippers. His things.

DAVID. Don't they only give you that when someone dies?

Beat.

IRIS. Shush.

Beat.

DAVID. Did he say anything? Before.

IRIS. What's that?

DAVID. Granddad. Did he say / anything?

IRIS. About what?

DAVID. Dunno. Anything.

IRIS. No.

DAVID. No?

IRIS. No, just mumbling. Bumbling. Not words.

DAVID. Nothing.

IRIS. No, I thought he was drunk standing there. Well, he was drunk; he'd been out all day – down the club he was with old do-da. What's-his-name. Halesworth. Holdsworth – Mike Holdsworth – wasn't he? And you know what he is with his driving gloves, and his hairpiece and… flash, he is. And course I spoke to your granddad in the afternoon – he said they'd only played a few holes, the pair of 'em, and well… the taxi didn't drop him home till gone ten. You could smell it on him apart from anything else. I mean, what am I supposed to think?

Beat.

David.

DAVID. Yeah.

IRIS. What am I supposed to think?

Eight

RITA*'s living room, early evening*.

RITA, *well dressed, and* DAVID.

DAVID. You're in his phone as Chuck.

RITA. Am I?

DAVID. Why?

RITA. Sorry?

DAVID. Why Chuck?

RITA. Oh. My name… My, my married name is Berry.

    Beat.

    He was a, a musician.

DAVID. I know who Chuck Berry is.

RITA. Yes.

DAVID. You're married?

RITA. Not… no, not quite.

DAVID. My granddad is. Divorced?

RITA. No. No, widowed.

DAVID. So that's what paid for this place?

RITA. Sorry?

DAVID. How long have you been…?

RITA. What? Here?

DAVID. What?

RITA. Living…

DAVID. Why would I care about that?

RITA. I don't know.

DAVID. I don't.

RITA. No.

DAVID. I wouldn't. I'm talking about you and my granddad.

RITA. Oh, yes.

DAVID. So?

RITA. Um…

DAVID. Um…?

RITA. A long time.

DAVID. How long?

RITA. Harry was – my husband was… he died almost seven
    years ago, so…

DAVID. Jesus.

RITA. No, it's not *nearly* that, but… two? Um… three.

DAVID. Three / years.

RITA. Your grandfather was – *is* – he's… he's been very good
    to me.

DAVID. I bet he has.

RITA. He has.

DAVID. That's what I said.

RITA. Have they said anything? The doctors? About…
    recovery, or…?

    DAVID *shrugs*.

    What, they're not – they're not, they're still unsure?

DAVID. It's none of your business.

RITA. Then, forgive me… why are you here?

    Beat.

    How is he, David?

DAVID. No, don't do that.

RITA. Don't do what?

DAVID. Don't use my name.

RITA. How should I address you?

DAVID. You shouldn't.

RITA. Fine. Then tell me how your grandfather is, and where I can see him, and you can leave.

DAVID. Oh, can I? Thanks.

RITA. I know it's upsetting.

DAVID. They said he's lucky to be alive so yeah, you're right, it is a bit. You should be a psychologist.

RITA. He's lucky to be alive?

DAVID. Yeah. It's not a word I'd use.

Beat.

He came here, didn't he?

RITA. When?

DAVID. Last night.

RITA. Yes, he did.

DAVID. And?

RITA. He was fine. He was wet, he'd walked here, but…

DAVID. What did he say?

RITA. Say?

DAVID. Yes, say, what words did he use?

RITA. I don't… I'm not, um…

DAVID. What?

RITA. I don't remember.

DAVID. You're lying.

RITA. No.

DAVID. Why are you lying?

RITA. I'm not.

DAVID. What? What did he say?

RITA. The usual – he, he wanted a drink.

DAVID. Why?

RITA. Because, that's what he does – and yes, because you
    knew about our... you knew about us.

DAVID. What else did he say?

RITA. You want every word?

DAVID. Just give me the highlights.

RITA. He said that he felt he'd wasted his life.

Beat.

DAVID. Is that it?

RITA. 'It'?

DAVID. Nothing else?

RITA. Such as?

DAVID. I think you know.

RITA. I'm afraid I don't.

DAVID. Did he leave you?

RITA. Leave me?

DAVID. You heard.

RITA. He left.

DAVID. You know what I'm talking about.

RITA. No, he didn't.

DAVID. Then what?

Beat.

What? Come on.

RITA. You'd rather not know.

DAVID. Then why am I asking?

RITA. He'd decided he was going to leave your grandmother.

Beat.

Where is he, David?

DAVID. Did he love you?

RITA. You mean… does he love me?

DAVID. No, you haven't seen him. I mean did.

Beat.

RITA. I think so.

DAVID. You think so?

RITA. Yes. I do.

DAVID. Did he tell you?

RITA. Well…

DAVID. Did he say it? The words.

RITA. I / don't think…

DAVID. Every day – morning, noon and night – did he tell you?

RITA. No.

DAVID. No?

RITA. No, / he…

DAVID. What, never? Not once?

RITA. Some things you know.

DAVID. You think you're…? What? You somehow think you're
    qualified to, to know all about him – to visit him even?

RITA. Yes, I am. I think / I am.

DAVID. You're not.

RITA. I wouldn't expect you to understand, David. Not with the life you've had.

Beat.

DAVID. Can I ask you something? Do you feel like a cunt?

RITA. Excuse me?

DAVID. A cunt. Do you feel like a cunt?

RITA. No, I don't.

Beat.

DAVID. You should.

Nine

Hospital room, night. FRANK *wired up to myriad tubes and machines.*

IRIS *sitting at* FRANK*'s bedside.*

RITA *in the doorway.*

RITA. Sorry.

She makes to leave.

IRIS. Eh?

RITA. S – Sorry. I / said…

IRIS. Right. What for?

RITA. What for?

IRIS. What are you sorry for?

RITA. For… Wrong room.

IRIS. Is it?

Beat. RITA *looks at her.*

RITA. Sorry, is it what?

IRIS. The wrong room.

RITA. Y – Yes.

IRIS. You're looking for someone else?

RITA. Yes.

IRIS. In a different room.

RITA *nods.*

You're not looking for my husband?

Beat.

I said, you're not looking for my husband?

RITA. No.

IRIS. Because if you are, here's what's left of him.

Beat.

What's the matter? You look a bit peaky.

RITA. No, I'm...

IRIS. You didn't think he'd managed to keep you a secret [did you]? I'm his wife, dear, he couldn't fart in the next room without it being written on his face.

RITA. I'm sorry, I... I shouldn't have come.

IRIS. No. No, I'm pleased you did. He hasn't had many visitors – any visitors, in fact. You're the first. Me, but I don't count, I'm his wife. And David, but David's family – and family aren't visitors, are they, they're family. But you're not. And here you are.

RITA. How is he?

IRIS. How does he look?

RITA. Is there a, a prognosis?

IRIS. You won't remember me.

RITA. Is he / recovering?

IRIS. I remember you.

RITA. Perhaps I should go.

IRIS. No, you won't – you'll stay there.

RITA. I'll – maybe I'll come back.

IRIS. You bleedin' well stay where you are.

Beat.

I remember you from twenty-odd years ago. When Frank
and I would go to the club – when he first went, this is. He
took me in those days, see, before Barbara – he told you
about Barbara, I take it? His daughter? Our daughter? He
told you about her?

RITA. Yes.

IRIS. Well, you know then; this is before she went – and we'd
still go out... and you'd be there at the dinners – you and
your husband. Your husband Harry. Harry Berry. Beautiful
couple, you were, everyone said. Always immaculate. Hair.
Clothes. And he'd speak from time to time, wouldn't he?
He'd get up and speak, and everyone would listen. I expect
you remember that?

RITA. Of course.

IRIS. I expect you miss that, do you?

RITA. Yes, I do.

IRIS. It's a shame, what happened to him.

RITA. Thank you.

IRIS. Shame they had to cut his face off. Especially as he died
anyway.

Beat.

We were there, at the funeral. Both of us. And the wake, we were at. At the club again, of course. You had salmon – smoked salmon.

RITA. Yes, we did.

IRIS. Frank was annoyed because you'd bought it from Crosbie's and not him, but I don't suppose he'll have told you that.

RITA. No.

IRIS. And as we went, as we left, I came over – we'd never spoken – and I said I was sorry for your loss. Something like that. I said, 'I understand it must be a difficult time'... and you looked at me like I'd spat on you. Like I'd said something vile. And you said, 'He's my husband,' you said. 'You couldn't begin to understand.' Just like that. Poisonous, like that.

RITA. I don't remember.

IRIS. No. Well no, why would you? Why would you remember? You had more important things on. You were his wife, I was a nobody. Wasn't I? I was a nobody to you.

RITA. I'm sure I / didn't intend to...

IRIS. Just like you are here.

Beat.

I know what he told you. Frank. I know what you thought he was going to do when he got home – he'd worked himself up into a right state about it. Pissed as a newt, of course. But he would never have gone through with it.

RITA. Is that so?

IRIS. Pie in the sky, dear – he knows where his bread's buttered. The last compos thing he did was apologise to me.

RITA. That's not true.

IRIS. Course it is.

RITA. I know that it's not.

IRIS. No, you don't know anything – not the first little thing. I met him on a market stall when I was seventeen years old. I'm his wife, dear. Who are you?

Beat.

That's right, no one. So you couldn't begin to understand, could you?

Beat.

Close the door behind you, there's a good girl.

PART TWO

One

Four months later. Morning.

A room in a care home. Fully furnished with a television, stereo, cupboards, curtains, bed, and the armchair from the golf club.

FRANK, *propped up with cushions in his chair. He is being fed from a drip through a 'peg' in his stomach.*

Some 'Dick and Dom'-fronted show is on the television in front of him.

He stares glassily at DAVID, *who is standing in the doorway with a large rucksack on his back.*

DAVID. Hello.

Beat.

You're in my chair.

He smiles.

Nice place. I like what you've done with the dry rot.

He drops the rucksack on the floor.

How's things?

No response from FRANK.

Yeah? That good? Me too.

FRANK *looks back to the television.*

I went to the National Gas Museum. That's an hour of my life I'll never get back. Thanks for that. What are you watching?

DAVID *swings round to have a look and sees Dick and Dom.*

What's that on for? You don't want to watch that, do you? You definitely don't want to watch those fucking idiots, they'll rot your brain. Sorry. Here.

He takes the remote and switches off the television.

Better, isn't it?

FRANK *looks to* DAVID. *His lips move, but he makes no sound.*

Hello.

Beat.

Sorry it's been a while... it's not that easy to get back. Turn's out it's not just a piss-up. And I've... I've sort of met someone, so. Ha. 'Met someone.' But I sort of have. We were gonna spend the break together. The whole thing, Christmas and everything, but... I said I wanted to come down and see you instead.

Beat.

For the conversation, mainly.

Beat.

I got you something.

He goes into his bag and rummages.

Bit early, but I thought you might fancy a bit of cheer.

He finds a Santa hat and puts it on FRANK*'s head.* FRANK *stares up at him.*

It's a good look.

He smiles and pats him on the shoulder. Thinks about giving him a kiss on the head... but kisses his fingers and touches them to FRANK*'s forehead instead.*

Beat.

DAVID *goes and gets a packet of cigarettes from his bag.*

Where's Nan? She left you?

FRANK*'s lips move.*

Yeah? Fair enough. You're not offering much to the relationship these days, are you? Bit of dribbling, but… Not much call for that. She does it herself when she hasn't got her teeth in.

Beat.

You've got a bit now, just…

He indicates his chin. FRANK *continues to stare blankly.*

Yeah…

DAVID *gets a tissue from somewhere and, though slightly repulsed, tries not to show it as he wipes* FRANK*'s mouth.*

There you go. You probably did that to me once, eh? When I was… little.

He regards his granddad staring at him, utterly helpless. Shakes his head, fighting it.

(*Sotto.*) Fuck.

IRIS *shuffles in with a cup of tea and sees* DAVID *looking down at* FRANK.

IRIS. Well…

DAVID. Oh, for / f…

DAVID *starts and hides his cigarettes.*

IRIS. Look who it is.

DAVID. You scared the shhh… the poo out of me.

IRIS. Oi.

DAVID. What? I didn't say / shit.

IRIS. Language. Come here – what's he got on his head?

DAVID. I brought it back with me.

IRIS. Give us a kiss then. He looks like a wally.

DAVID. Well… yeah.

IRIS. You've made him look like a silly boy.

He kisses her on the cheek.

DAVID. I don't think that's the hat.

IRIS. Well, it's not going to help, is it, I tell you that much.

DAVID. He likes it.

IRIS. Does he?

DAVID. Said he feels festive.

IRIS. Take it off. Go on.

DAVID *does as he's told.*

Let me have a look at you, then.

DAVID. Come off it.

IRIS. You look like you've lost weight.

DAVID. I haven't.

IRIS. Do you want a biscuit?

DAVID. No.

IRIS. I've got biscuits.

DAVID. I'm fine.

IRIS. Or chocolate?

DAVID. I'm not hungry.

IRIS. Have a Penguin.

DAVID. No.

IRIS. Or a Wagon Wheel.

DAVID. I don't want / one.

IRIS. You've lost weight.

DAVID. I haven't!

IRIS. You have.

DAVID. I've only been gone about five minutes.

IRIS. Long enough to start smoking, wasn't it?

DAVID. What d'you mean?

IRIS. David. You'll have to go outside if you want one of them.

DAVID. It's alright, I can wait.

IRIS. It's what caused this, you / know.

DAVID. I know.

IRIS. You'll end up like him [if] you're not careful.

DAVID. Well. I'll be careful then.

IRIS. You better had. [If] there's one thing you don't want to end up, it's him.

Beat.

DAVID. How's he been?

IRIS. Oh, you know, doesn't dance like he used to. He's a better listener, I'll give him that.

DAVID. Has anyone been in to see him?

IRIS. No, no one, no, not a peep.

DAVID. Really?

IRIS. Not even a bunch of something from the club, or old what's-his-name with the hair. Hepworth.

DAVID. Holdsworth.

IRIS. Him. Still, he doesn't want them to see him like this, does he?

DAVID. I suppose not.

IRIS. No. Of course not.

Beat.

DAVID. He was watching Dick and Dom when I came in.

IRIS. He what?

DAVID. Dick and Dom, these two… morons. Kids' TV. They're the presenters, but… Anyway, he was sitting there watching them like it was *Newsnight*.

IRIS. The golf must've finished. I had the golf on for him.

DAVID. I thought he might learn to use the remote.

IRIS. So did I.

DAVID. Has nothing improved? Since I last spoke to / you.

IRIS. Like what, love?

DAVID. Speech or… movement or anything?

IRIS. No, the little speech girl says it's more or less a waste of time, the amount we have her. Reckons there's nothing she can really do an hour a week, so that's that…

DAVID. So why doesn't she come more often?

IRIS. Eh? And who's going to pay for that? No, that's extra – once a week, that's it, that's all they give you. Which is a shame 'cause she's a nice girl. Scottish. Or Irish, she is. Irish. Does the dancing. Pretty little thing – you should try and meet her. Monday mornings she / comes.

DAVID. I'm alright thanks.

IRIS. Well, you say that. As for moving about – the physiotherapist comes twice a week – Tuesdays and Thursdays – but all that does is stops him getting worse. But you can see how his legs have started wasting, look, where he's not using them.

DAVID. Is that the best they can do?

IRIS. Well, it's what they all get, isn't it? I did try to get him some cognitive something-or-other, but it's fifty pound a bloody hour, so.

DAVID. So he gets three hours' treatment a week.

IRIS. Most weeks.

DAVID. That's shit.

IRIS. Oi.

DAVID. Well it is.

IRIS. Well, that's how it is.

DAVID. But... if he was rich he could have loads.

IRIS. Well...

DAVID. He'd be walking by now.

IRIS. I don't know about that.

DAVID. He wouldn't just be getting worse.

IRIS. We shall never know, will we?

Beat.

DAVID. Have you tried getting a loan?

IRIS. What for?

DAVID. For more treatment.

IRIS. Who's going to give me a loan?

DAVID. The bank?

IRIS. No.

DAVID. It's worth a try.

IRIS. No, I did try. I did, I tried; I looked into it.

DAVID. And?

IRIS. Well... I've got no way of paying them back, have I?
They can't lend me any money because I don't make any, I
haven't got a pot to piddle in. He'd have been alright if his
pension wasn't a couple of buttons and a ball of string – I
mean, I tried to tell him, / but...

DAVID. Is there anyone else you can ask?

IRIS. Like who?

DAVID. I dunno...

IRIS. No, I think we're just waiting now, to be honest, love.

DAVID. Waiting for what?

Beat.

FRANK's hand goes to his middle and takes hold of the feeding tube through his shirt at the point where it enters his stomach.

IRIS. Here we go. Watch him.

IRIS speaks to him as if speaking to a disobedient dog.

Leave it. Frank… Frank. Leave it.

FRANK's grip relaxes a little but his hand stays where it is.

Properly. Leave it.

DAVID. What's he doing?

IRIS. He keeps trying to pull things out. (*To* FRANK.) Frank.

DAVID. What things?

IRIS. Anything, you name it – his favourite's his wee bag. A while ago they found him in the morning with it all – (*To* FRANK.) leave it.

DAVID. Why would he do that?

FRANK grips the tube again and starts pulling. His face remains expressionless, serene.

IRIS. He gets – right…

IRIS goes and holds on to FRANK's hand.

Let go. He gets uncomfortable, wants the tubes out. It's worse at night for some – let go.

FRANK just looks at her.

Frank.

He pulls harder.

Do as you're told.

He shows no signs of letting up as IRIS *tries to prise his fingers away from the tube.*

David.

DAVID. I'll get someone.

IRIS. No, come here.

DAVID. I'll get a / nurse.

IRIS. Come here and help me.

DAVID *goes over.*

DAVID. What…?

IRIS. Hold his arm.

DAVID *takes hold of* FRANK*'s arm.*

(*To* FRANK.) Do as you're told.

DAVID. Granddad.

IRIS. No. / Frank.

DAVID. Fuck me, he's strong.

IRIS. Language.

DAVID. He is though!

IRIS. Stop bleedin'…

DAVID. Granddad.

IRIS. Frank. Stop it. Stop – ! Pinch him.

DAVID. What?

IRIS. Pinch him under the / armpit.

DAVID. I'm not gonna pinch him.

IRIS. He won't stop otherwise. Do it.

DAVID. No.

IRIS. I'll do it.

DAVID. Don't pinch / him.

IRIS. It's the only way to get him…

> IRIS *starts pinching him.*

DAVID. It'll hurt.

IRIS. Well, that's the point, isn't it?

DAVID. It's cruel.

IRIS. 'Cruel.' Here.

> *She pinches harder.*

He's a grown man.

DAVID. Well, yeah, but…

IRIS. Stop it, you stupid old sod.

> *She twists her hand.*

> FRANK *groans faintly and stops straining. His hand relaxes.*

> IRIS *and* DAVID *let go of him.*

There. Now leave it.

> FRANK *looks to his armpit, as if looking for the source of his pain.*

DAVID. Look – you've hurt him.

IRIS. Well, what do you think'd happen if he pulled his peg out?

DAVID. They can just put it back in, can't they?

IRIS. It can take hours for them to get round to doing that. And in the meantime, what? He bleeds and gets infected. He's got to learn, hasn't he? Otherwise they'll just strap him to the bed.

DAVID. What, really?

IRIS. Course they will. They haven't got time to patch him up all day long. I made him these, look…

She goes to the bed and takes something from under the pillow. It's a pair of knitted mittens, except they have no thumbs to them: they're more like thick woollen bags that are rounded at the end and taper at the wrist.

…to stop him doing it overnight – pulling things out, or off, or… He has to have his oxygen on at night, you see, because he's lying down, so his chest has to, what's it, work harder – they haven't got enough staff on to keep an eye on him all night – so I made him these so he can't grab at anything.

DAVID. Show me?

He takes them, looks them over.

IRIS. I dropped a few stitches.

DAVID. You did this?

IRIS. They don't even know about them, I shouldn't think.

DAVID. This place is gash.

IRIS. Well, like I said, it's the best we can do.

She takes the gloves and puts them back under the pillow.

DAVID. How much is it to go private?

IRIS. Oh, I don't know, varies. The cheapest anywhere here was something like three-thousand-odd a month.

DAVID. Jesus / Christ.

IRIS. There's a brochure somewhere. Three thousand, three hundred and something. I know, so you can put that out of your head.

DAVID. That's…

IRIS. I know it is.

Beat.

DAVID. He's paying for me, isn't he?

IRIS. What's this?

DAVID. He's paying for me to be at uni – his / money.

IRIS. Oh, don't worry about that, that's alright.

DAVID. But he could get treated with that, couldn't he?

IRIS. No, that's yours, he saved, he wanted you to have that.

DAVID. That was before / he had...

IRIS. No, no, no, don't start all this – that's put away for you to do your university and get yourself a certificate. End of.

DAVID. But it's his money.

IRIS. It's not, it's your money and I don't want to hear anything more about it. Besides, it wouldn't make a dent. It'd get him a couple of months' worth of whatever, / then...

DAVID. Better than nothing.

IRIS. No, then he'd have to give it up and he'd be right back to square one, no better off than he is now. No, I'll keep on buying my lottery tickets and you use that to do something with your life. Just make sure you don't waste yourself. Alright?

DAVID. That's...

IRIS. What?

DAVID. No, it's funny. He said the same thing. Just before...

IRIS. What did he say?

DAVID. 'Don't waste yourself.'

IRIS. Well, there you go – great minds.

DAVID. Yeah.

IRIS. Eh?

DAVID. Yeah.

Beat.

I'm gonna... I'm going outside for a bit.

IRIS. Alright, love.

DAVID. Won't be long.

IRIS. Don't have more than one. And have a look at the thing on the packet. The pictures. That could be you, / see.

DAVID. Thanks.

IRIS. Well. Go on then.

He goes.

IRIS *turns, picks up the remote control and flicks on the television.*

Dick and Dom's show plays. IRIS *watches a moment, squares* FRANK *up to the television and pushes him closer.*

There you go. Dick and Dan. I don't know which is which. But they're watching you now, so you behave yourself.

Two

The same room, a day or two later. Late afternoon.

FRANK *propped up in the chair, which is now facing away from the television. The drip has been replaced by an oxygen mask.*

RITA, *close to him.*

RITA. You read about them, don't you? People who go off. Away. And they check into a hotel… just as though it were a normal hotel, with coffee and tea and… bed linen. And chocolates on the pillows. Like a holiday. Like they were just going on holiday. I suppose they are, in a way.

Beat.

We could've gone away, couldn't we? If you'd wanted to. We could have found ourselves a swimming pool with a bar in it. Margaritas and…

Beat.

Of course, you have to sign something. Before. You must sign to say that's what you want when... You would have signed, wouldn't you? If you'd known.

Beat.

Still, here we are. Here we both are. Aren't we? Frankie. There you are.

Beat. She looks off. Looks back.

I've missed you.

She kisses his hand. DAVID, *entering with a cup of tea, catches this.*

DAVID. Sorry.

RITA *stands.*

RITA. No...

DAVID. I couldn't remember if you said sugar, so... I didn't put any / in.

RITA. That's fine, thank you.

DAVID. I can go back if...

RITA. No, that's... That'll be fine.

DAVID. Are you sure?

RITA. Thank you.

DAVID. Did you ask for sugar?

RITA. It really doesn't / matter.

DAVID. Because I don't mind...

RITA. It's fine, really. Let's just... leave it, shall we?

DAVID. Okay.

Beat.

There's Penguins...

RITA. Sorry?

DAVID. Or Wagon Wheels? Blue Ribands? If you want / something sweet.

RITA. Oh. No. Thank you.

DAVID. My nan. She says they're for visitors, but I think she's the only one who comes here, / so.

RITA. Yes, I suppose she is. Where is she now?

DAVID. Doing a shop.

RITA. Can we expect her?

DAVID. No. I mean, yeah, but not for ages, so.

RITA. I see.

DAVID. She's gone to the Tescos near us. Apparently the one round the corner hasn't got Viscounts. These mint things he used / to like.

RITA. I know.

DAVID. Yeah.

RITA. Very thoughtful.

DAVID. Well, it's her who's going to eat them.

RITA. So she won't know I've been here?

Beat.

DAVID. How is it?

RITA. I still haven't tried / it.

DAVID. No, I mean… seeing him. How is it?

Beat.

RITA. He looks thinner.

DAVID *smirks*.

DAVID. You sound like her.

RITA. Do I?

DAVID. Well, no, but…

RITA. Good.

Beat.

How is he?

DAVID. You mean apart from…?

RITA. Apart from the obvious, yes.

DAVID. Erm… Not great. I mean he's got these sores from not moving. These bed sores. From the chair. And the bed, obviously.

RITA. How often is he up and about?

DAVID. Well, that's it – never, really. A couple of times a week when the physio comes. And on top of that he gets this thing with his lungs where he can't swallow, so they have to be drained with this machine. Which is…

RITA. It sounds awful.

DAVID. It's not nice. But if they don't get drained his breathing gets worse and he needs the mask – like now. I mean, it's mainly at night, / but…

RITA. So they've not been in to see him for a while?

DAVID *shakes his head.*

And when will they come?

DAVID. I dunno.

RITA. When will they do his draining?

DAVID. Tomorrow?

RITA. Why not today? / If he's…

DAVID. They might, but… There's just not enough staff – I mean, it's not their fault but he only gets checked on every few hours and even then – most of them are just babysitters, so.

RITA. You mean they're not nurses?

DAVID. Some of them are, but…

RITA. But not all of them.

DAVID. There's this porter who comes in – he seems to like him – but he's a porter, so what can he do?

RITA. That's not… that can't be standard?

DAVID. It's the NHS.

RITA. Even so.

DAVID. It's sort of been fine 'cause my nan's been here, but it's a lot of work.

RITA. I can imagine, yes.

DAVID. And he keeps trying to pull out his tubes and…

RITA. And it's not good enough. Carrying on like that.

DAVID. No, yeah, exactly.

RITA. So why hasn't your grandmother moved him elsewhere?

DAVID. Well, this is it – we can't afford it.

RITA. Why should it cost you?

DAVID. To go private, I mean. It's three grand a month.

RITA. He could just go to another – a better – state home.

DAVID. But you don't get to pick, is / the thing.

RITA. Of course you do.

DAVID. No, they just put you somewhere and that's it.

RITA. Who do?

DAVID. I don't know. The health authority.

RITA. Is that what she told you?

DAVID. Who? My nan? Yeah.

RITA. Why here then?

Beat.

If it's the health authority that chooses the home, then why has he been sent here? There are tens of care homes exactly like this one nearer to where you live.

DAVID. I don't... Places, I suppose.

RITA. Places?

DAVID. Yeah, availability, yeah. Free places.

Beat.

RITA. I used to visit him at the hospital, when he was there. I thought – I didn't think your grandmother knew – not after the first time at least. I'd leave it late until I knew she had gone. Some nights I even saw her driving out... then one evening I went, as I always did, and he just, he... he wasn't there. He'd been discharged.

DAVID. To here, yeah.

RITA. But they wouldn't tell me where he'd gone. They wouldn't say – only that he *had*. Because I wasn't next of kin, they said. And because they had been asked 'not to disclose'.

DAVID. By...?

Beat.

RITA. So, I went to the golf club to see if they knew. Had anyone spoken to your grandmother, or... been to see him...? Nothing. Some of them didn't even know he was ill. Then Poirot – Jeanie – the barmaid, she said that she'd seen your grandmother the day before. For the first time in years she had come into the club with two men in polo shirts – a van outside – and without so much as a word to anyone they picked up his chair and carried it out. And that was it. He disappeared.

Beat.

DAVID. So...?

RITA. So it's not the health authority, David. He's miles from home and impossible to find. He's being hidden away.

DAVID. No, why would – ? Why? What for? No, it'll just be places.

RITA. Has anyone else been to visit?

Beat.

Cards? Flowers?

Beat.

So she's had him all to herself, hasn't she?

DAVID. He wouldn't want people to see him like this.

RITA. He hasn't had much of a choice.

DAVID. What does he have much of a choice in? Somebody's got to decide.

RITA. Do you have any idea what it's like, David?

DAVID. Any idea what what's like?

RITA. Being completely apart from the single most important person in your life.

Beat.

DAVID. Maybe, yeah.

Beat.

RITA. Is that why you asked me to come?

DAVID. No. I mean… No.

RITA. Then why am I here, David? After months of being kept away what exactly is it I'm doing here?

DAVID. I've… Look, I've…

Beat.

Yeah, I've got a sort of proposition.

Three

The same. Evening.

IRIS, DAVID, RITA *and* FRANK *– who becomes increasingly distressed as the scene goes on.*

IRIS. He's not a fucking timeshare.

DAVID. Nan.

IRIS. I'm not going to rent him out.

DAVID. I'm not / saying that.

RITA. He's not your commodity to rent.

IRIS. Course he – in this situation that's exactly what he is.

DAVID. It's not like / that.

IRIS. A 'commodity' – he's my bloody husband.

RITA. Yes and don't I know it.

IRIS. Then you should bleedin' well know to / keep your oar out.

RITA. I've spent the last three years suffering because of it.

IRIS. Good.

RITA. He's spent the last forty-something.

IRIS. How dare you / bloody…

RITA. Do you know what he told me?

IRIS. Get out – how bloody dare you?

RITA. I dare because I'm right!

IRIS. Are you balls.

RITA. He needs this – what I am offering – *I* am thinking of him.

IRIS. Well, that'll make a change, won't it?

RITA. I have every right to help him get back to / being as he…

IRIS. You have no right. None whatsoever.

RITA. Look at him! Is that what you want? He is still in there somewhere, Iris.

IRIS. And he's still mine.

RITA. He doesn't belong to you!

IRIS. Well, he sure as bloody hell doesn't belong to you.

RITA. And shutting him up in here won't make him fall in love with you if that's / what you're trying to do.

IRIS. There's that word again.

RITA. Treating him like he's a baby – like you're his mother.

IRIS. He's seventy years old, he doesn't need love!

RITA. What?

IRIS. He needs to be warm, he needs to have a roof over his head and his wife to tend / to him.

RITA. He needs physiotherapy.

IRIS. He gets it.

RITA. He needs cognitive therapy, he needs tongue and speech therapy, he needs to be able to swallow, and eat for himself / eventually.

IRIS. I'm not stupid.

RITA. He needs stimulation and interaction, not four beige walls and a television set.

IRIS. Well, this is what he's got.

RITA. It's not good enough. He needs a quality of life, Iris – and you are denying him that to serve some / warped sense of…

IRIS. We're his family. Us. Not you.

RITA. It's not about family!

IRIS. Then what's it about?

RITA (*simultaneous*). It's…

DAVID (*simultaneous*). It's about getting Granddad the care he needs.

IRIS. You keep out of it. (*Back to* RITA.) We don't need your money.

RITA. I'm not offering it to you.

IRIS. We don't need anything from you.

DAVID. We do, Nan!

IRIS. Keep out, I said. (*To* RITA.) You had your chance with your own husband and you ballsed it up, / and now you –

RITA. You don't have the faintest idea.

IRIS. Now you want to try and run mine? Well I'm sorry…

DAVID. It's not – Nan, that's nothing to do with it – Mrs Berry can give him / a better…

IRIS. Mrs Berry now, is it?

DAVID. She can give him more of what he needs. It's not going to help him, keeping him here – he'll just get worse and worse…

IRIS. Enough!

DAVID. …until eventually – that's it – and it's not fair.

IRIS. 'Fair'?!

DAVID. Not when he could be somewhere that'd look after him properly.

IRIS. Don't talk to me about fair – I will not share my husband.

DAVID. It's not – you wouldn't be sharing; you'd visit on your own like you always do and whenever you weren't there…

IRIS. She'd be looking after him.

DAVID. Someone else would be with him. It's the best thing for everyone.

IRIS. Not me, it's not. I let a woman steal my husband away from / under my nose.

RITA. I'm not trying to steal him! If you'd listen you'd see that I'm trying to help him, which is something you've clearly given up on.

IRIS. I'm here all hours of the bloody day and night, don't you tell me I don't care.

RITA. If he went to a private home you wouldn't have to be here – he'd get proper supervision, with regular checks / and...

DAVID. And he might pick things up – learn to swallow and hold stuff... move around.

IRIS. And?

DAVID. And all it would mean is arranging separate times for the two of you to visit – give him a chance, Nan, please.

Beat.

IRIS. No. No, what, he goes somewhere fancy, gets all the treatment under the sun and she goes to visit him willy-nilly? Then what? What, he gets better?

DAVID. Maybe.

RITA (*simultaneous*).Yes.

IRIS (*simultaneous*). Then what? He's up, he's walking, he's talking, what happens then?

DAVID. He goes home.

IRIS. Does he?

Beat.

Or where does he go?

RITA. That's up to him.

IRIS. No, it's up to me, he stays here.

DAVID. Nan.

IRIS. He stays here – (*To* RITA.) and you keep clear. You keep well away, if I so much as hear you've been near the place I'll have the police on / to you.

DAVID. Nan, you've got to at least –

IRIS. The pair of you. I mean it.

DAVID. What?

IRIS. Get out.

DAVID. Nan!

IRIS. Both of you, you as well. If you think he can do without me, well, you'll see.

Beat.

Out, I said!

They stand there, staring at IRIS, *who is trembling.*

Beat.

RITA. I will be doing everything I possibly can to get him transferred to a private care home and out of this council-run pit, Iris. In the meantime, I will visit as and when I like. You can call the police, but they'll laugh you off the telephone.

IRIS. Get out.

Beat. RITA *goes to* FRANK. *She takes his hand.*

RITA (*whispers*). I'll see you soon, Frankie.

She kisses his hand.

I'll be in touch, David.

DAVID. Yeah.

IRIS *just stares at the ground ahead of her as* RITA *exits.*

Nan…

IRIS. It's no wonder your mother took one look at you and buggered off for good.

Beat.

DAVID. What?

IRIS. I'd've killed myself an' all.

He grits his teeth and, just about swallowing it down, walks out.

Silence.

Eventually, IRIS *looks at* FRANK.

That's the worst thing I've ever done.

Four

The same. A week later. Early afternoon.

FRANK*'s chair is occupied by a black bin liner full of clothes.*

On the floor are a couple of biscuit tins and some odd chocolate bars.

DAVID *is crouching down with another bin liner, clearing a cupboard.*

He reaches in. Takes out a couple of drinking mugs and puts them in the bin liner.

Reaches in again. Takes out a stack of old newspapers.

Reaches in again. Stops.

DAVID. Jesus Christ...

He takes out a handful of Twixes or something and puts them in a pile with the others.

(*Of* IRIS.) This is why you've got no fucking teeth.

*He carries on putting the remainder of the cupboard contents
into the bin liner: newspapers, brochures, a pair of pyjamas.*

*He ties the sack, collects the other from the chair and
deposits them by the door.*

Just as he does so, RITA *enters, pushing* FRANK *in a
wheelchair. He is in a dressing gown, pyjamas and slippers.
His hair is wet.*

There you are. I was starting to think you'd gone under.

RITA. They were quite rough with him.

DAVID. Were they?

RITA. He wasn't happy.

DAVID. I bet.

RITA. He coughed up some blood.

Beat.

DAVID. Yeah. He's been doing that.

RITA. Still – it's done now, isn't it? He won't have to put up
with it again. And at least he'll be clean when he gets there.

Beat.

Did you leave us some clothes out?

DAVID. Yeah, there's one of everything in that drawer. Except
for shoes, they're over there.

RITA. Thank you.

DAVID. Will you be here in the morning then?

RITA. Of course. Will you?

DAVID. Yeah. I'm on a twelve o' clock train, but.

RITA. And is your grandmother coming?

DAVID. No. I mean, I doubt it. I haven't really spoken to her
since…

Beat.

I heard her the other day. In the kitchen.

Beat.

I think she was crying.

Beat.

RITA. He will be better off, David.

DAVID. Yeah. Yeah. I know.

Beat.

RITA. So you'll make it back to Leicester for Christmas Eve?

DAVID. Yeah. It's a bit weird… I've never spent it with anyone else.

RITA. There's a first time for everything.

DAVID. Yeah.

RITA. Does it all feel a bit too grown-up?

DAVID *smiles.*

DAVID. No.

Beat.

What are you doing?

RITA. No plans as yet. There's a carol concert on Christmas morning, perhaps we'll go to that. Apparently some of the nurses sing.

DAVID *nods.*

Beat.

DAVID. Thank you.

Beat.

RITA. Thank you.

Beat.

DAVID. Do you want a Viscount?

RITA. Sorry?

He collects the tins and chocolate bars.

DAVID. A Viscount. The mint things.

RITA. Oh…

DAVID. Or a Twix, / or…?

RITA. No, thank you. I'm actually, I'm allergic to chocolate.

DAVID. Yeah?

RITA. I'm afraid so, yes. Always have been.

DAVID. How unlucky are you?

RITA. Oh, I don't know.

DAVID. Well… I'll just leave these for the staff, then. A present.

RITA. Very nice.

DAVID *smiles and exits with the biscuit tins in his arms.*

RITA *and* FRANK *remain. She goes to her handbag. She produces a CD and puts it into the stereo as* FRANK *watches.*

The same song they danced to in Part One plays softly. RITA *sits by* FRANK *and sways, humming along to the track.*

After a while, IRIS *appears in the doorway with a holdall.* RITA *stops as she sees her. She switches off the music.*

IRIS. I wanted to see him before he goes.

RITA. Yes. You can see him after as well, if you like.

IRIS. No.

Beat.

RITA. Well, I shall leave you to it.

IRIS. Before you go…

Beat.

Did Frank ever…?

RITA. What?

IRIS. Did he tell you…?

Beat.

Because he didn't with me. Not once. Not in forty-odd years.
I thought he *did*, you know, I thought he must have felt some
sort of – something to start with at least – or else why
bother? Why bother in the first place? But he didn't say it.
And I didn't even realise, you know… I never realised he
hadn't, not until Barbara… And he got up in the church and
he talked about how much he loved her. He'd written her a
poem, well, I'd never known him to write his own name.
Something about breathing. About her being like oxygen. He
barely got halfway through it. And I wondered – did she ever
know? And I thought to myself – what a tragedy to go
through life and not know a thing like that.

RITA. Yes.

IRIS. I used to think perhaps that was why she did it, you
know…

RITA. It must have been very lonely.

IRIS. Oh… it has been, dear. Yes. It has been.

RITA. I meant / for her.

IRIS. You meant for Barbara, course you did.

RITA. I did, yes, but…

IRIS. I expect he'll have said it to you, did he?

Beat.

You can say.

Beat.

RITA. Yes. He did.

IRIS. Did he?

Beat.

RITA. I'm sorry.

IRIS. What for?

RITA. Lots of things.

IRIS. No. All's fair, isn't it? In…

Beat.

RITA. Perhaps not.

IRIS. No.

Beat.

I brought him some clothes. Smart ones.

RITA. Oh?

IRIS. If he's going to go, he should be wearing a tie.

Five

The same. That evening.

FRANK *in the wheelchair, facing the television.*

IRIS, RITA, *and* DAVID *all watching* You've Been Framed *with* FRANK. IRIS *is by his side, holding his hand.* RITA *is the other side of him, at a distance.* DAVID *on the floor.*

A pile of FRANK's *clothes, including a tie, laid out on his wheelchair.*

All except FRANK *laugh occasionally at the clips.*

IRIS *is nodding off.*

A clip of an elderly woman falling over / off a swing / hitting someone with a golf club / whatever.

DAVID. That's like you, Nan.

Beat.

Nan.

He turns around to see that she has fallen asleep. Beat.

Right…

He gets up and gathers their things.

RITA. Are you off?

DAVID. Yeah. I think we probably should.

RITA *switches off the television.*

RITA. I shall follow your lead.

DAVID. Nan? Nan. Time to go.

IRIS. No, I'm alright here for the minute.

DAVID. I think maybe we should get off. I still need to pack. And Granddad's got a long day tomorrow.

Beat.

IRIS. Alright then. If you want.

She stands and DAVID *makes to help her on with her coat.*

No, leave that, I'm alright. It's mild out tonight. There's something lovely about it.

DAVID. Let's get you to bed then, shall we, Granddad?

FRANK *stares back at them emptily.*

Yeah…

He starts to get him up out of his seat.

IRIS. Here, let me help.

RITA. I'll do it with / you.

DAVID. No, it's… no. It's fine, I think I've got him.

He manages to pick him up and carry him, like a babe-in-arms, to the bed, where he lays him out.

There you go.

RITA. His air.

She finds a small kit somewhere with oxygen tank and mask.

DAVID. Thanks.

IRIS. I'll finish off putting him to bed. If you don't mind.

DAVID. Yeah.

RITA. Of course.

DAVID. I'll... wait downstairs. See you in the morning, Granddad. Sweet dreams.

He kisses his fingers and touches them to FRANK*'s head.*

I'll be by the machine. (*To* RITA.) And see you tomorrow.

RITA. Yes, see you then. Can you be persuaded, Iris? Tomorrow?

IRIS. I don't think so, dear.

DAVID. Are you sure, Nan?

IRIS. Yes. I am, I'm very sure, thank you.

DAVID. Right.

Beat.

IRIS. If I could have a minute.

DAVID. Yeah...

RITA. Goodbye then, Iris.

DAVID *goes.*

Goodnight, Frank. Sleep well.

Beat.

Let me know if you change your mind.

She nods her goodbye and RITA *exits.*

IRIS *looks down at* FRANK *on the bed, who in turn looks up at her.*

She covers him up with a sheet, pulling it up to his chin.
Takes the oxygen mask and gently places it over his mouth.
Switches it on. It begins its low hum and hiss of air.

She softly lifts up his head and reaches under the pillow for
the 'mittens'. She holds them in her hand. Looks at them.
Looks at him.

She moves away and places them inside her bag.

Across the room she looks back at him, and he at her.

She opens her mouth to speak.

Doesn't.

Beat.

IRIS. Just so's you know… I wouldn't change my lot.

She continues to look at him.

She nods to herself and leaves, switching the light off.

A few moments of FRANK *alone and helpless in the*
moonlight.

Six

IRIS'*s hallway, night.*

DAVID*'s rucksack by the telephone table.*

Silence.

The phone begins to ring.

Beat.

A light flicks on from the bedroom.

A few moments, then IRIS *shuffles into the hallway in her*
dressing gown. Stops by the bedroom door, barely awake.

She shuffles across to the ringing phone, places her hand on it.

Beat.

She withdraws the hand. Looks at the ringing phone. Backs away from it.

It stops ringing, but she continues to look at the phone.

A few moments.

It starts ringing again.

DAVID, *half-asleep, arrives from another door in a T-shirt and underwear.*

He looks across at his grandma, who just stands there staring at the phone. He looks to the phone himself and they both just watch it ring. Eventually, IRIS *looks at* DAVID.

IRIS. Well, that's that then.

And she slowly returns to her bedroom.

The ringing continues. DAVID *looks at the phone. Moves towards it.*

He puts his hand on the receiver.

Beat.

Snatches up the receiver to his ear.

The End.

A Nick Hern Book

Goodbye to All That first published in Great Britain in 2012 as a paperback original by Nick Hern Books Limited, 14 Larden Road, London W3 7ST, in association with the Royal Court Theatre, London

Goodbye to All That copyright © 2012 Luke Norris

Luke Norris has asserted his right to be identified as the author of this work

Cover image by feastcreative.com
Cover design by Ned Hoste, 2H

Typeset by Nick Hern Books, London
Printed in the UK by Mimeo Ltd, Huntingdon, Cambridgeshire PE29 6XX

ISBN 978 1 84842 259 9

A CIP catalogue record for this book is available from the British Library